The how and why of this book

Every day of the year thousands of teenagers access the Dr Ann website (*www.teenagehealthfreak.org* and *www.doctorann.org*). Many of you who check out the website email us questions about your health and other problems in your life. These are about a whole range of issues – sex, drugs, relationships, weight, bullying and stress. This book contains the questions which come up most often, and our answers to them.

The *www.teenagehealthfreak.org* website was originally set up because of the success of the books *Diary of a Teenage Health Freak* and *The Diary of the Other Health Freak*, both published by Oxford University Press. If you look at the website, you can catch up with the latest on Pete Payne and all his worries about his spots, his girlfriend and all the rest in his day-to-day diary. Or you can read the books – whichever. And now you, like Pete Payne, can also find out what worries teenagers and how to get the absolute best answers – by reading this book. It is mainly for young people aged around 13 and over, though many adults will learn a thing or two!

AIDAN MACFARLANE is a consultant paediatrician and public health doctor who ran the child and adolescent health services for Oxfordshire. He is now a freelance international consultant in teenage health.

ANN McPHERSON is a general practitioner with extensive experience of young people and their problems. She is also a lecturer in the Department of Primary Health Care at the University of Oxford, where she runs the DIPEX research group on patients' experiences of health and illness.

As well as *The Diary of a Teenage Health Freak* and its sequel *The Diary of the Other Health Freak*, their other books include *Mum I Feel Funny* (which won the Times Educational Supplement Information Book Award), *Me and My Mates*, *The Virgin Now Boarding*, and *Fresher Pressure*. They also published a book for parents about the teenage years called *Teenagers: the agony, the ecstasy, the answers*. The authors also run the extremely successful website on which this book is based – *www.teenagehealthfreak.org* - which receives around 250,000 hits a week and was the winner of the BUPA communication award.

Authors' acknowledgements

We would like to thank: all the teenagers who emailed us – whether we were able to answer them or not – and all their parents for having them (the teenagers) in the first place. Once again, we would like to thank Liz, Charlie and the rest of the team at Baigen for their wonderful work on the website; Mike and Jane O'Regan for all their past support and their funding.

Note

The answers we have given to the questions in this book are based on our personal clinical experiences as doctors when dealing with similar clinical problems. Young people reading the book will, we think, be helped by the answers we have given. However, it is impossible for us to offer advice in such a way as to deal with all aspects of every individual's health problems. Therefore, if you, as a reader of this book, have any continuing doubts or concerns about your health problem, we would strongly advise you to consult your own medical practitioner.

To preserve the true flavour of the original, we have not changed or edited the language or spelling of the emailed questions used in this book. However, in the few cases where real names are used, these have been changed to protect the anonymity of the senders.

the
tRutH

a teeNager's suRvivAl guiDe

Aidan Macfarlane  **Ann McPherson**

OXFORD
UNIVERSITY PRESS

Great Clarendon Street, Oxford OX2 6DP

Oxford University Press is a department of the University of Oxford.
It furthers the University's objective of excellence in research, scholarship,
and education by publishing worldwide in

Oxford   New York

Auckland   Cape Town   Dar es Salaam   Hong Kong   Karachi
Kuala Lumpur   Madrid   Melbourne   Mexico City   Nairobi
New Delhi   Shanghai   Taipei   Toronto

With offices in

Argentina   Austria   Brazil   Chile   Czech Republic   France   Greece
Guatemala   Hungary   Italy   Japan   Poland   Portugal   Singapore
South Korea   Switzerland   Thailand   Turkey   Ukraine   Vietnam

Oxford is a registered trade mark of Oxford University Press
in the UK and in certain other countries

British Library Cataloguing in Publication Data

Data available

ISBN 978-0-19-272703-9

Contents

· · · · · · · · · · · · · · · ·

Stress

1

All about
Stress

Our lives are full of changes and stress. They often go
together. Stress is what we may feel as we try to adapt
or cope with changes – changes at school, family changes,
work changes, physical changes like puberty, relationship
changes, and more.

On the good side, a bit of stress gives us the buzz to cope
with these changes. The changes that happen inside us
from having to cope with changes outside can make us
more aware of life and help us feel more confident about
dealing with the future. So the right amount of stress can
be good for us. It can add to our excitement about life and
make us feel stronger.

By far and away the best advice on how to deal with stress comes from young people themselves. They are experiencing the stress and they know the best ways of coping with it. In this part of the book the advice and experience of young people are given without replies from Dr Ann: all the advice has been emailed to us by young people who have been through the stress themselves.

TALKING TO OTHER PEOPLE

'I feel it's important that you get some feedback on the subject of stress as it effects so many people nowadays and I feel that reading about similar situations can sometimes help someone else get through this difficult stage. Throughout my secondary school years I had such a terrible time and I didn't feel like I could open up to anyone. It took 1 individual to spoil what's supposed to be the best time of your life. Hardly seems fair does it? Endless times I sat talking to myself, deciding how I would react the next time I came face to face with this monster?! Yet somehow I never followed my actions through and I tried to ignore her torturing comments and endless abuse. It was horrific! I couldn't walk past her without her making a comment or childishly throwing herself into me. Her evil glares made me feel so small and I constantly asked myself why me? I do consider myself to be a decent person – I wouldn't hurt anyone, not even her. But why? She was stabbing at me through her words and actions. She hacked away at my emotions, sending *them crazy. I was completely trapped. I felt so alone. Still to this day I have never opened up to anyone. I try and hide this terrible time of my life but it will always be with me. Always. It's important to know that you are not alone and somehow there is always a light at the end of the tunnel. It will save you. Remember that!'* **GIRL AGED 17.**

* *

'You *can beat being stressed by always talking to someone – maybe more comfortable talking to friends or one of your own relations.'* **GIRL AGED 11.**

* *

'I *think you should try and talk to someone trusted about your problems because a problem shared is a problem halved! I always found it quite hard to do that at first but when you confide in someone you feel a weight has been lifted off your shoulders and you no longer hold the weight of the world on your back.'* **13 YEAR OLD GIRL.**

* *

'My *friend takes his anger out on me every day at school. He has temper, memory, hearing and eyesight problems. He calls me names and makes me really stressy. I take my anger out on myself sometimes but not very often. Best is that I talk to my dad sometimes and sometimes my friends, which helps me.'*
BOY AGED 14.

EXERCISE

'**If** I'm stressed I go swimming, which releases the chemicals from my brain.' **GIRL AGED 11.**

· ·

'**If** you are stressed, you need time out to think about things, so you should go for a long walk or something to clear your head. Or talk to someone you can trust like your parents or close friends.' **GIRL AGED 12.**

THINKING YOURSELF OUT OF IT

'**I** reckon you should just think of the good things in life and don't let it get to you, or just have a good cry and get over it.' **GIRL AGED 14.**

· ·

'**If** you are stressed out then you should go out and do something that you really, really enjoy so as to take your mind off things.' **BOY AGED 13.**

· ·

'**Stressing** about your work doesn't help at all. I find that if I stress out and worry I end up not doing anything. The truth of it is that if you think something is really hard at school, then everybody else does too. We just have to say to ourselves that we will do our best and that's all that matters.' **GIRL AGED 16**

'**You** need to forget about everything that's going to happen and take things as they come.' **GIRL AGED 15.**

· ·

'**Just** tell ya self you can get through tests, SATs etc… and if you are being bullied stand up to them. I found most bullies are all mouth.' **14 YEAR BOY.**

MUSIC

'**Go** up to your room and put on some calming music and when you feel calm enough, go and talk to the person that stressed you out.' **GIRL AGED 16.**

· ·

'**Go** upstairs, whip some big headphones on, close ur eyes, lie on ur bed n listen to the best music you have.'
BOY AGED 14.

BEING ON YOUR OWN

'**The** best way 2 cope with stress…is probably just to be on your own once in a while, somewhere quiet so you can think.'
15 YEAR OLD GIRL.

· ·

'**If** you are stressed out, just chill in your room and watch TV. It works for me.' **GIRL AGED 11.**

· ·

OTHER WAYS

'**If** I have loads of stuff to do (homework or too much other stuff) then I get REALLY stressed out. To tackle this I write down a list of all the things I need to do to remind me and I cross it off as I do it. It really helps!!!!' **GIRL AGED 13.**

'**What** do you do if you are getting stressed by being bullied?
1) tell a parent
2) tell a friend
3) tell a teacher
4) tell them to leave you alone
5) just ignore them.' **14 YEAR OLD GIRL.**

'**Take** natural remedies, herbal teas, and read lots of good books while listening to a bit of light classical music – that does it for me.' **17 YEAR OLD BOY.**

'**There** are a few things but the thing that really gets me is when I try 2 train my dog! She mostly listens 2 me but when she doesn't I take it out on her by shouting at her! So I take her on a walk and she suddenly makes me O.K. again. She does it with all my stresses.' **GIRL AGED 12.**

'**If** ur stressed go out n live life a little!! if ur parents want u 2 stay in & revise then stay in, but only for 4 nights of the week cuz otherwise it aint fair on u!!' **GIRL AGED 15.**

EASY THINGS TO DO

Dear Doctor Ann, *What are the five top things to help stress?* **BOY AGED** 13.

Dear *'Stressed' – Any number of things cause stress. A bit of stress is perfectly normal and something that we all have to put up with – it probably even helps us get things done! However, too much stress does stop us functioning properly. Here are some tips to help:*

- *make a list of things that are stressing you*

- *talk to a friend, your parents or another adult about what is stressing you*

- *look at the individual things that are stressing you, and only attempt to deal with them one at a time*

- *do something you really enjoy, to give yourself a break from the things that are stressing you*

- *take some exercise, as this helps release the natural endorphins in your body, which will help you cope with your stress*

- *a sixth one for luck – avoid too much caffeine, as in coffee, coke and tea, as too much of it can increase your feelings of anxiety*

Dear Dr. Ann, *I think that when people get stressed they should have a go on a punch bag – is that OK?* **GIRL AGED** 13.

Dear *'Have a go on a punch bag'* –
Thanks for this suggestion. I agree that
sometimes it can help to deal with stress
by punching something. Just make sure it
is a punch bag or a pillow or a
cushion or something soft, so that
you won't hurt yourself when you
hit it. Also make sure that it is not
another person, so that they
won't get hurt or hurt you back!

WHEN FEELINGS OF STRESS ARE WORSE

Doc – how do you get rid of horrible memories that you get
nightmares about? **13 OLD YEAR BOY.**

Dear *'Having horrid memories that you have nightmares
about'* – This sounds serious, and something that you need to
talk to someone about over a period of time. Memories serious
enough to give you nightmares will finally fade, but they can be
eased by talking through your feelings about these memories
with a counsellor. And if that doesn't work, you may need to see
a psychiatrist. First off, I would suggest that you go and talk to
your family doctor.

• •

Dear Doctor Ann, I get this dark, angry feeling
when I'm upset or angry. Maybe it's stress but I
really need advice on how to stop this feeling,
sometimes it makes me cry. Please help!
13 YEAR OLD GIRL.

Dear *'Dark angry feelings'* – Yes, maybe this is stress. It does sound as though talking to someone about your feelings would help you. Have you tried doing this? Other things that you might find help are suggested by other young people who get really stressed. They suggest things like listening to music, going for a walk and writing things down. If your feelings are making you cry, you definitely do need to tell someone else about them, so that they can get you help. It is not good holding these feelings inside you. Other people can help.

• •

Dear Dr, what should I do when I'm really stressed???
13 YEAR OLD GIRL.

Dear *'What can you do when you get really stressed'* – The first thing is to ask yourself, 'Can I avoid getting stressed in the first place?' What is it that is giving you the stress – friends? exams? teachers? overwork? Then you should ask yourself whether you can avoid any of these stresses. Some you will be able to avoid – maybe overwork or certain friends – but many you won't be able to avoid, like exams and teachers. Even more likely is that there will be several different things at any one time that are giving you stress, so a good thing to do is to make up you mind what all the stressful things in your life are and write them down. Then decide that you are going to try and do something about these one at a time. Suppose it is something like not getting enough sleep. Make the decision to go to bed earlier – have a hot bath before bed to help you relax, avoid drinking anything with caffeine in it, and try reading a restful book. If that works, then after a week decide on the next stressful thing that you are going to tackle.

Dear Doctor Ann, How can I stop feeling so stressed out when all I want to do is scream and smash something?
14 YEAR OLD GIRL.

Dear '**All I want to do is to scream and smash something'** – Actually screaming is probably not such a bad thing. Some people also find smashing things helps as well, but it is a good idea to be very careful about what you choose to smash and where you smash it. Old china that no one wants smashed outside in the back garden is the safest, but that still may upset your parents, so it is better to try and avoid getting to the stage where you want to scream and smash things. First, you need to understand what all the different things that are stressing you are. It is easy to let a whole range of different things get to you at the same time, and then together they feel so overwhelming that you feel there is nothing that you can do about them. And then it is SCREAM AND SMASH time – because you feel so overwhelmed. Well, if you look at each of the stresses separately, they may be more manageable. Dealing with a little bit at a time will give you a feeling that you are back in control again.

WHO TO TURN TO

Dear Doctor Ann, What should you do if you feel stressed and you need to talk to someone other than your mum or a friend? 15 YEAR OLD GIRL.

Dear '**Stressed but want to talk to someone other than your mum or a friend'** – There are other people around you who you should be able to trust and talk to about how you feel. There may be someone else in your family who is close to you – an aunt or uncle – or a family friend? If not, have you thought of talking to the school nurse or a teacher? Otherwise, why not go and see your family doctor? If you don't want to go with your mum, you can still arrange to go and see him/her by yourself. You don't have to have your parents with you, and the doctor will keep anything that you tell them secret unless they feel that you are in danger of being harmed in some way. And even then they will discuss who you would like told about it.

DO MEDICINES HELP?

Dear Doctor Ann, A question about stress… do you know of any medical ways of calming down stressed people?
14 YEAR OLD GIRL.

Dear *'Any medical ways of calming down stressed people'* – It depends what you mean by 'medical'. Normally doctors would first recommend that you try some of the self-help methods of dealing with stress. If that didn't work, they might then suggest seeing a counsellor or even a psychiatrist. But yes, there is a whole range of medicines which do calm people. However some of these also make people feel a bit like zombies – they don't have any strong emotions at all, it sort of does away with the 'passions' of life, which isn't always very helpful! A bit of stress is a normal part of life, and we all need to learn to cope with this kind of stress. The better we deal with this kind of stress, the more we are able to cope with the really big stresses, so you don't want to go rushing off to take medicines every time things go badly. But when the stresses are really, really bad – yes, medicines can definitely help.

Bullying

All about Bullying

It is difficult to know why we – young people and adults alike – have suddenly become so much more aware of bullying. We know that in our society physical violence is much less tolerated – with the abolition of caning in schools and the move to stop children being smacked, even by their parents. Although bullying has never really been acceptable, there has also never been a time when people have been so acutely sensitive to the need to stop it from happening.

One of the problems with bullying is that it takes so many different forms. Often, what is happening is obvious to both the person being bullied and to the person doing the bullying. But sometimes you may be unaware that you are being bullied but just know that you are being made to feel unhappy. Sometimes you may bully others without being sensitive enough to know that you are bullying. At other times your 'teasing' may overstep the mark and become bullying – it can be difficult to know where to draw the line. What we do know is that making other people's lives miserable by bullying should not be allowed to happen. What is also obvious is that most of us experience bullying at one time or another in our lives, and that many of us will also be bullies at one time or another.

THE WHAT, WHO AND WHY OF BULLYING

Hi Doctor Ann. *What is bullying?* **14 YEAR OLD BOY.**

Dear *'What is bullying?'* – Bullying is when someone or several people do or say nasty or unpleasant things to you, or keep on teasing you in a way that you don't like. Almost everyone gets bullied by somebody at sometime in their lives. Sometimes it's hard to tell where teasing ends and bullying begins. Bad bullying is bad enough even if it just happens once, but it when it goes on and on it can become a serious problem.

Dr Ann – *Why do people bully other people?* **13 YEAR OLD BOY.**

Dear *'Wanting to know why'* – *People bully others for a whole range of different reasons. Some people don't feel good about themselves and they put other people 'down' in order to feel 'up'. To do this they may tease or taunt other people about lots of different things. These include: the way they look; the colour of their skin; how hard they work; if they have a physical or mental problem of some kind; if they come from another country; if they wear spectacles or have braces on their teeth. Bullies pick on almost anything, as long as they sense that they can make another person feel bad about themselves, or at least worse than the bully feels about himself or herself. Many bullies are people who were bullied themselves and the only way they can feel better is to do it to another person. Understanding this can be helpful to someone who is being bullied and might also stop them from becoming bullies themselves.*

BULLYING FOR NO REASON

Ann – *hi I was bullied a lot last year for no reason at all, it just all started one day. I was getting really upset and did not tell anyone but it kept on going on. When I was being bullied I was kicked, punched, spat at and everything you could think of. I was even scared to come to school and walk home.*
GIRL AGED 14.

Dear *'Bullied for no reason'* – I guess the reason these bullies were kicking and punching you was to look big themselves and seeing you scared made them feel powerful. Frequently bullies will try to make someone else miserable because it makes them feel better. It helps them with their own feelings of lack of confidence if they can see they can make someone else feel the same way. If you don't show any signs of giving in – then they usually give up (though they may go and find someone else to bully instead).

NAME CALLING

Dear Doctor Ann, I am being bullied by some people in my form at school. They aren't hitting me, they're just calling me names and it really hurts. **14 YEAR OLD GIRL.**

Dear *'Being bullied'* – There is an old saying: 'Sticks and stones may break my bones but names will never hurt me'. In fact I do not think the saying is true, as being called names is a really nasty form of bullying and often very difficult to deal with. Try to ignore the name-calling, though I realize this may be hard. Bullies get their pleasure from seeing that they are upsetting you. Link up with other friends so that you don't feel isolated. It does sound as though you are being made depressed by these bullies. Don't keep it all to yourself. Please tell your parents who can talk to your teachers. Some schools have special systems for dealing with bullies.

THREATS AND VIOLENCE

Dear A – *a girl at school has been threatening me online saying that I will be beaten up by the end of the week and when I go to secondary school. I thought it was just talk but today she started bumping into me and elbowing me when she walked by. My mom and I are having a meeting with the Head, but I don't think she'll do anything about it. Should I go to her mom or the police to have it on file? Please help me. My grades and family life are being affected by this. Thank you.* **13 YEAR OLD GIRL.**

Dear '**Threatened online**' – *Threatening people using emails, mobile phones and text messages is just a new way of bullying. Schools are all meant to take notice of pupils being bullied – whatever way the bullying is being done. I would suggest that you try to get the school to take this up before involving the police. Other practical things that you can do are – change your email address, block emails coming through from that particular person or from their mobile phone number. Remember to keep a copy of all the abusive emails so that you can really show people what has been happening – if you need to.*

SUICIDAL

Dear Dr Ann. *I need some help. I am lonely in the world and nobody loves me because I have a lot of spots and my last girlfriend said my willy was too small. Everyone thinks I am a geek and it is going round that I am gay. What should I do? I really want to leave school and I have been thinking of suicide. PLEASE HELP ME!* **17 YEAR OLD BOY.**

Dear *'Suicide thinker'* – I think that you need help from someone very quickly. The question is who would you find it easiest to talk to about this? Have you tried talking about the way that you feel with someone that you trust and who is close to you – your parents, a teacher or a doctor? Don't bottle these feelings up inside you – talk to other people about them. Think positive! First deal with the spots – your doctor can give you some medicine for them – so that is one thing out of the way. Next – at least you have had a girlfriend (even if she was mean). Try to ignore the negative comments from others. Listen to, and think about, the positive things about yourself.

FRIENDS?

Doc – a group of my 'friends' are quite horrible to me and make me feel crap about myself and life and make me want to die. Should I leave the group and make new friends? I've considered this before but am scared they will be really nasty to me if I do.

15 YEAR OLD GIRL.

Dear *'Person with horrid friends'* – Yes, dump these so-called 'friends' now. You don't need them if they are making you feel like crap. Don't be scared, be positive and self-confident and think about the fact that there will be many, many people who want to be your friend because you have so much to offer. There will be genuine friends out there who make you feel good about yourself – go find them.

BEING GOOD AT WORK?

Dr Ann – *I was bullied in school because I always done my work and they used to make me cry. Every one called me a cry baby but when I told my mum she made me go and tell the head teacher and she made it stop.* GIRL AGED 13.

Dear *'Person being bullied for doing their work'* – *The people who bullied you were probably just envious of you for doing well so they wanted to make you suffer too. You seem to have dealt with this sensibly by yourself – well done – it shows that if you tell someone about being bullied you can get it stopped.*

LIKING DIFFERENT THINGS

Dear Doctor Ann *I think I am totally different from everyone else at school and listen to classical music and play an oboe at grade 8! Everyone teases me for this. Is there some way i can boost my self-confidence?* 15 YEAR OLD GIRL.

Dear *'Oboe player'* – *Hang in there and stick with the oboe playing. Your friends may tease you now but you will be in huge demand in the near future as the world and orchestras are desperately short of good oboe players. Also there are lots of brilliant guys around in orchestras who, like you, are into the classical stuff.*

STANDING OUT FROM THE CROWD

Dear Dr. Ann *I get bullied because I look different to every one else so every one picks on me including the teachers at school. What do I do?* 15 YEAR OLD GIRL.

Dear *'Person who looks different and gets picked on'*

— Here are two ideas for ways of dealing with this problem from other people who have been bullied. Joe suggests: 'Stand up to the bullies. Don't walk past them with your head down and a grim face. Walk past, holding your head up high and smiling, and be confident. Show them they don't hurt you (even if they do). Don't lower yourself to their level, if they call you names don't get mad or call them back just laugh it off and walk away — show them they don't bother you.' Liddy says 'I am being bullied at the moment. I usually twist their words round to go against them or turn what they say into a compliment. It works. For instance, if they said "You're a geek", I'll say, "I'm a geek and proud of it!" They can't really say anything back to that in my experience!'

BULLIED – FOR SEX

Dear Doctor Ann, my boyfriend keeps bullying me into sleeping with him what should I say to him?
14 YEAR OLD GIRL.

Dear *'Person with a bullying boyfriend'* — You don't want to sleep with this boy, so say NO. If he does not hear the first time say NO again and again until he both hears and believes you. There are lots of other things you can say, like it's illegal, that you are too young, etc., but the main reason is you don't want to and that should be enough. I know it sounds corny, but if he really likes you he won't leave you just because you won't sleep with him.

NO ENTRY

BECAUSE OF THE COLOUR OF YOUR SKIN

Dear Doctor Ann, *I am an Asian living in a predominantly English area. I get beaten up and spat at even by people younger than me. I can't speak to anyone because they wouldn't understand. I feel really down and cry a lot because of it. Who can I tell and what can I do?* **15 YEAR OLD GIRL.**

Dear *'Person being beaten up and spat on'* — *This is racist behaviour and totally out of order. You should tell your parents, teachers, friends — anyone you feel comfortable talking to. You should find that they'll all be sympathetic about this bullying. Unfortunately, ganging up together against others who are in some way different than themselves seems to make some inadequate people feel good. Try to find a friend who will support you — and go with you when you go out anywhere. It doesn't matter whether they are Asian, white or any one else as long as they are not racist, are against bullying and are on your side. Remember there are lots of people who are very strongly anti-racist and anti-bullying whatever their colour or race.*

WHEN BULLIES WANT TO STOP

Doc *— I have never been bullied but I do bully. I'm 14 yrs old and myself and 3 other girls bully another girl. We all hang around together, even the girl that we bully, and she is our friend but we are all nasty to her. We pick on her and say nasty things to her. I wish we would stop. We have all tried to be nice to her but we just can't. We've even tried to get rid of her by falling out with her coz we hate hurting her so we thought she should find new*

friends but she just cried. So we had to make friends and we're still being nasty to her. Plz help me!!!!!! **GIRL AGED 14.**

Dear *'Bullier'* – *What is outstanding here is that you realize what you are doing and can be so open about it. That has to be a beginning. But why do you do it? What kind of satisfaction does it give you? Does it make you feel good and powerful – being able to make someone else miserable? Does it make you feel that you can't be bullied yourself, if you are bullying someone else? You obviously can put yourself in your victim's shoes, so that you understand what it would be like to be bullied. You don't want this, so put an end to it now. Maybe you and your friends should get together and talk to this girl and explain that although you can stay friends, it might be better for her to find some new mates to hang out with who she would get on better with and who would be nicer to her.*

IGNORE THE BULLIES

'When *I was bullied I just ignored what everyone said, no matter how hard it was. I let them do it, because all bullies want is a reaction and if they don't get it they stop bullying.'* **BOY AGED 15.**

'When *I first started at my school, I had loads of 'friends' but after a while they started being nasty. They kept pushing me and tripping me up but the worst of all they called me names. Sometimes I just cried in my room but I knew I had to do something about it. One day at lunch they decided to do it again but I didn't let them I just ignored them and carried on with my* life. A few days later they came up to me and asked to be my friend, I said 'no' and walked off. Now I found some new friends, and the old ones don't come near me anymore.' **GIRL AGED 14.**

• •

'**I** used to get bullied. They would call me lots of names like 'fat' bitch and 'ugly' bitch – it was not nice but then I said to myself 'bullies are cowards'. Don't let them bring you down – just have confidence in yourself. I said that and ignored them and my friends also help me know it is true. Now I don't get bullied anymore and I have more friends than ever and I am happy. So anyone getting bullied don't let them get ya and don't let them see you are upset about it. That just makes them happy and they will keep at ya.

15 YEAR OLD GIRL.

TELL SOMEONE ELSE ABOUT IT

'**I** was bullied in primary school from the age of 7 to the age of 10. I was always big for my age but I had lots of friends and so I was happy with myself until a few kids in the year above started saying I was 'fat' and a 'cry baby'. It really upset me and so I became isolated from my friends and just wanted to be alone. I didn't want my friends to see me upset. My mum began to see that something was wrong with me and one day she saw me sitting alone crying. She came into the school and I finally told her what was wrong. She convinced me to go and tell my teacher who was really kind and supportive and she had a quiet word with my bullies. After that they each wrote a letter to me saying sorry and I didn't have any more trouble from them.'

Weight

Eating too much
Eating too little

Many, many young people get stressed about what they eat and the way they look. Food can make you fatter or thinner, and it can also influence how tall you end up, how strong you are, and lots of other things as well. But – and it's a big BUT – it is not always easy to get the food right or the right food. The best you can hope for is to get most of what you eat right most of the time.

HEALTH, EATING AND DIET

Dear Doctor Ann – *what is the difference between healthy eating and dieting?* **BOY AGED 14.**

Dear *'Healthy eating or dieting'* – *Healthy eating is more a matter of putting good food into your body, while in dieting the focus is more on cutting out 'bad foods'. Best is to go for the good foods from the start! But not too much of anything.*

IS THERE A PERFECT DIET?

Dear Doctor Ann – *What is the perfect diet?*

GIRL AGED 15.

Dear *'Person wanting the perfect diet'* – *You mean the perfect diet to stay thin? The perfect diet to enjoy food? The perfect diet to avoid getting heart disease when you are older? The perfect diet to make sure you get all the essential foodstuffs to grow and avoid getting too fat? If you eat a range of healthy foods and don't eat too much of any of them, then your body will tend to sort out what it needs. So what do we mean by a 'healthy' diet rather than a 'perfect' one? While you are growing, you do need lots of energy, but most young people in the UK choose too many foods that have too much fat and sugar. For vitamins and minerals, a healthy diet should include five portions of fruit or vegetables a day, so get counting! You also need some fish, meat, cheese or beans (for the protein and fat), pasta, bread or potatoes (for energy), as well as a bit of fat from milk, cheese and other dairy foods. Food manufacturers tend to put too much salt and sugar in many of their snacks and foods because that's what they think people will buy, but if you are used to snacks with lower sugar and salt, they taste just fine.*

Hi – *how can I lose weight the easiest way?*
GIRL AGED 11.

Dear *'Person looking for easy way'* –

Start by looking at what you are eating by keeping a diary, and you will soon see how you can change what goes into your mouth so that you become healthier and lose weight at the same time. If you are eating lots of fatty foods, cut down on those and eat more fruit and vegetables, as they have fewer calories in them. Try and eat smaller portions of whatever you do eat. Eat regular meals so that you don't get too hungry. And don't try and lose lots of weight all at once – go slow and steady, losing half a pound/quarter of a kilo a week is fine. You should also look at how much exercise you are taking. You should be doing at least 20 minutes a day – enough to make you sweat, though it doesn't matter whether it is swimming, running, dancing, football or whatever. The table below gives an idea of how much exercise you need to do to 'burn off' various kinds of yummy stuff. In rough terms, 60 minutes of moderate cycling, 60 minutes of dancing, 50 minutes of swimming, 30 mins of running – all use up about 200 calories.

Yummy stuff	Number of calories	Moderate exercise needed to 'burn it off' (minutes)
Chocolate bar	281	85
Bag of crisps	184	55
Can of Cola	139	42

WORKING OUT YOUR IDEAL WEIGHT

Doctor Ann – *what weight should I be?* BOY AGED 12.

Dear *'What weight should I be'* – *There is quite a wide variation in what a 'normal' weight is for any one person. This normal range depends on whether you are a boy or a girl and how old you are. So the right/normal range for you as a boy aged 12 obviously isn't the same as for a girl aged 15. To see the right range of weight for you personally, look up your age on the weight chart for boys given overleaf. It is only a guide – if you want a more accurate way of finding the correct weight for your sex, height and age – your so-called Body Mass Index (BMI) – then go to www.teenagehealthfreak.org and click on 'Body Mass Index' in the A–Z index. You will be asked for your age, height and weight, and then it will automatically calculate your normal weight range.*

GIRLS

Age (years)	Weight (kg)			Height (cm)		
	Low normal	Middle	High normal	Low normal	Middle	High normal
10	24	33	50	126	139	151
11	26	37	55	130	144	158
12	29	40	60	135	150	164
13	33	45	65	142	155	170
14	37	50	70	147	160	173
15	40	54	74	150	162	175
16	43	56	76	151	163	176
17	44	57	77	152	164	176
18	45	58	78	152	164	176

BOYS

Age (years)	Weight (kg)			Height (cm)		
	Low normal	Middle	High normal	Low normal	Middle	High normal
10	24	31	46	126	139	151
11	25	34	52	130	143	157
12	28	38	57	134	147	163
13	30	43	65	140	155	171
14	35	49	72	146	162	179
15	39	55	80	153	169	185
16	44	60	85	158	173	188
17	48	64	88	161	175	190
18	51	66	90	165	176	190

Dear Doctor Ann – *How many calories can I eat a day?*
GIRL AGED 16.

Dear *'Wanting to know about calories'* – Calories measure
the amount of energy that is contained in different foods.
We all need to eat enough food to have enough energy to
do all the things we want to do, but the body also needs
calories just to tick over – even if we just lay in bed all day!
The more active we are, doing exercise like running and
swimming, the more calories we need to take in in our food.
So I can't tell you the exact amount of calories you need,
but the table below gives you some guidance. In general, boys
need more calories than girls, but in the end it comes down to
how active you are.

	AGE (years)	Approximate daily energy requirement (calories)
BOYS	**9–11**	2200
	12–14	2640
	15–17	2880
GIRLS	**9–11**	2050
	12–14	2150
	15–17	2150

FAT FOOD EFFECTS

Dear Doctor Ann – what does eating fatty foods do to my body? **BOY AGED 15.**

Dear 'How do fatty foods affect my body'
– You are probably worried about fatty foods because you hear all the time that they are bad for you. It is true that some of them are better than others. But eating some fatty food is absolutely essential, especially for children and young people who are growing. Fat provides energy, helps insulate your body and keep it warm, and is a vital part of many cells in your body. Fat also makes some foods taste better. Some vitamins which we all need, such as A, D, E and K, can only be absorbed into our body when combined with fat. BUT fat is full of calories. There are about twice as many calories in each gram of fat, like butter or cheese, as in carbohydrate foods like bread. Too much fat in your diet, especially from meat and cheese, can make you fat.

FAT FEARS, FADS, FANTASIES...

I am really worried about my weight, every time I have something to eat I get paranoid that I am going to put on weight by eating it. HELP. **GIRL AGED** 14.

Dear 'Worrier about your weight' – I know how you feel. But we all have to eat in order to survive, and that is far, far more important than worrying about being overweight. Food should be fun after all. If you take exercise as well as eating a fairly healthy, normal diet – with five pieces of fruit or vegetable a day and no bingeing on choccies, etc. – you should be fine.

• •

Dear Doctor Ann – I only eat potato, cheese, bread, fruit, chocolate and a few other things. But I am quite healthy and not underweight (8.5 stone/54 kilos). Is this bad for me? I can't eat other things – if i try i panic and it's really getting me down, as i can't go out with my friends and stuff. **BOY AGED** 14.

Dear 'Panicking over food' – The fact that you are healthy and your weight is normal does mean that whatever you are eating is not doing you much harm in the short term. It sounds as though you are getting a mixture of the basic foods, carbohydrate, protein, fat and vitamins. But it does sound as though you have a bit of an eating problem if you can't eat with your friends and panic if you have to eat certain foods. Try making a list of them and gradually try just a little taste of each one every day at home, until you can eat them normally. Once you can do this, you could try inviting a friend to eat with you at home and then try eating out with just one or two friends.

WEIGHT AS A WEAPON

Doc – *some people in my class tease me about my weight but I ask my friends and they say I am not fat. Why are these people bullying me?* **GIRL AGED** 13.

Dear *'Teased about your weight'* – *I am so sorry that you are being teased. No one, whatever their size or shape, should get bullied about the way they look. The best thing to do is ignore these stupid taunts. If you really want to find how you compare with others and what is considered your 'normal' weight, check out the chart on* **page 35**. *Or you could ask your doctor to check you out. There is an especially wide range of normal height and weight at the time of puberty. Your body is still growing and changing, so as long as you are eating healthily and taking exercise, you should have nothing to worry about.*

THERE IS 'MODEL' THIN

Dear Doctor Ann – *I'm told I'm pretty all the time by people I don't know, and I've even been told I should be a model by a modelling agent, but I'm still stressed about my weight and how I look. I eat really healthy and exercise for an hour every day but I haven't seen any changes in my size.* **PLEASE HELP**, *all I want is to be fit and happy with myself.* **GIRL AGED** 14.

Dear *'Wanting to be fit and happy'* – *You seem to be doing all the right things, eating healthily and exercising for an hour a day. That is very good, as is being pretty. A great many people want either to be models or to be like models, but you must remember that because of 'fashion', most models are abnormally thin. You are going to have decide whether you want to keep on worrying*

about your weight and the way you look all the time
– which could be a nightmare. Or you could just
decide to be fit and happy with yourself. That's a bit
more worthwhile than being a neurotic matchstick
clotheshorse. Is that really worth all the stress?

STRESS, SMOKING, EATING

What can you suggest because I find that I eat when I am
stressed and I want to stop as I am. **GIRL AGED** 12.

Dear *'I find I eat when I am stressed'* – *Yes, lots of people find
that they want to eat when they are stressed. It is probably your
body seeking some kind of comfort. Many people find chocolate
is a particular favourite for doing this, and it is thought that
chocolate does contain chemical substances that help stress.
The problem, as you already know, is that chocolate also contains
a large amount of sugar and therefore, when eaten in large
quantities, makes you fat. But another way of dealing with stress
is to take exercise. This helps the body to release chemicals
(endorphins) which help to calm stress,
and of course exercise also helps
you to lose weight rather than
gain it. Pick some kind of
exercise or sport which you
already enjoy, maybe tennis or
swimming or walking, and just
work harder at it. Around 20
minutes of exercise most days
of the week, if you can manage
it, is good for all these things.*

My friend is 14 and she says she smokes because it makes her not eat so she has stayed thin – is this what is causing it? GIRL AGED 15.

Dear 'Friend of a girl who's staying thin' –

Lots of girls start smoking because they think it will help them get thin, as well as making them look sophisticated and sexy. Smoking doesn't make people thin – it just costs a lot of money, makes your breath smell bad, and gets you hooked onto something which is very, very hard to give up. Your friend won't suddenly turn into a whale if she stops smoking, though some people do put on a few pounds when they first quit, partly because after a few days food tastes nicer. Tell her she's likely to lose it again, though some people who have cigarettes for pudding instead of a cream cake do find the weight goes on when they go back to the cream cakes. Suggest she eats some fruit instead. But many people who give up smoking don't notice any weight change at all – their body adjusts quite happily. If she quits, she'll look better, feel better and smell better, and with the money she saves, she will be able to afford to enrol in one of those classy gyms, keep slim and buy more clothes.

SKIP THE STRICT DIET

Dear Doctor Ann – What is wrong with me? I am having rapid weight loss – 6 kilos in 2 weeks as I have been on a very strict diet to lose weight as I think I am too fat. I can barely eat now as I don't feel hungry and feel very full, very fast. When I do eat my little amount of food, I have extreme abdominal pain about 5 minutes after, lasting anywhere from 30 minutes to hours. GIRL AGED 14.

Dear *'Losing weight very fast from dieting'* – *STOP DOING THE STRICT DIETING NOW, as otherwise you may have a real eating problem. The reason you don't feel hungry is because when you go on a very strict diet, you start to break down fat and protein in your body, and your body produces chemicals called ketones which tend to make you lose your appetite and to feel tired and not so well. The pain is probably because your 'guts' are not used to being starved of food for so long. Try to get back to eating normally, small amounts at each meal time, and then I am sure you will start to feel better. To lose weight, you need to diet sensibly and not lose more than about a quarter of a kilo (half a pound) a week. The best way to do this is by avoiding too many fatty and sweet foods. Cut down the size of your portions, eat fresh fruit and vegetables instead of sugary snacks and crisps, and try to do 20 minutes a day of some type of exercise that makes you sweat.*

• •

I'm *On a Diet. I Weigh 6 stone 12 [44 kilos] and im 13. every 1 Says im crazy but i think im fat! im now eatin an apple n a small plate of salad a day, is that enough? i dn't feel hungry! thank you 4 ure time x*

Dear *'On a diet'* – *Please stop dieting. Everyone is right – you are crazy if you think you are fat. Your weight is absolutely normal for your age. It is not enough to eat only an apple and a small plate of salad every day. You are in danger of developing an eating disorder by doing this. You need enough calories to grow properly. The best way to be fit and not fat is to eat a healthy diet and do some exercise.*

EATING DISORDERS

Dear Doc – *when I get stressed I eat and eat and eat, and then feel 'gusted with myself and make myself throw up by stuffin my fingers down my throat. I reckon it happens about three or four times a week. What should I do?* **GIRL AGED 15.**

Dear *'Eat and eat when you're stressed'* – *It sounds as if you have what is called 'bulimia'. The common thing that happens is that something like stress triggers you and you start gorging yourself on all those delicious things like cakes and biscuits and chocolate and stuff. Sort of 'comfort' eating. But then you feel disgusted with yourself and you make yourself vomit. The trouble is that you never vomit up everything that you have taken down, and that means that you tend to put on weight. Many people binge, then go on to be so disgusted with themselves that they become anorexic, and that is much more difficult to stop. So try to find other ways of dealing with your stress than eating yourself sick. First write down those things which are stressing you, and try and avoid situations where you get stressed. Next, when things get too much, find other distractions like going for a walk or ringing a friend. As far as eating is concerned, make sure that you sit down to regular meals with your family. You need to get proper help from the school nurse or your doctor before it becomes too much of a habit.*

I'm really confused. I think I could be depressed or something. I used to be anorexic for a while and got very skinny but now I seem to be overeating and indulging myself when I'm not even hungry. I want a way out of this, I'm sick of it. I would just like to stick at 9 stone [57 kilos] and stay there. I went on holiday and put half a stone on and now I have put even more on because of binge eating. I feel very upset and depressed and often cry about being so fat and disgusting. **GIRL AGED** 14.

Dear '**Was anorexic, now bingeing**' – The pattern of being anorexic and then binge-eating is called bulimia and is really quite common in girls. What happens is that when you become anorexic, you set very strict rules for yourself about what you can and cannot eat. These rules are usually so strict that you can't stick to them because you feel so hungry. So you have to break the rules by bingeing on everything you can lay your hands on. Then you vomit and try to get rid of all those extra calories you have just taken in. But the truth is that, however much you vomit, you cannot get rid of more than half the calories you took in during the binge, so people with bulimia tend not to lose weight. You really, really need to ease up on the dieting and think of other ways of keeping your weight under control – something sensible, though, not too drastic. The best way is to eat healthily, which simply means including in your diet each day five portions of fruit and veg (five in all, not five of each!). This will fill you with good stuff and help hold off feelings of hunger, so you won't eat too much of anything else. At the same time you need to take some exercise. Nothing drastic like running marathons, but just build in about 20 minutes of walking, swimming or some other form of gentle exercise every day.

ANOREXIA, ANOREXIA, ANOREXIA

What happens if someone is anorexic – could they die? How can you help someone who is anorexic? **GIRL AGED 15.**

Dear *'Wonder what happens to anorexics'* –

Fortunately many young people with anorexia do get better if they get help and treatment. They are most likely to recover completely if they get treatment as soon as the eating disorder starts. BUT some people do die from it if they get very very thin, usually because they upset all the chemicals in their body, which stops the heart working properly. If anyone you know has anorexia and is losing weight from very strict dieting, then please do try to persuade them to get help. Even if they tell you it's a secret, you must tell some adult you trust, who will be able to help sort things out.

Dear Doctor Ann – *I'm a veggie and my friends think that I am anorexic because I don't eat very much but I know that I eat loads really. What should I do, should I listen to them and eat more because I am fine about the food I eat and enjoy it.* **GIRL AGED 14.**

Dear *'Veggie'* – *Just because you are a vegetarian does not mean you are anorexic. However, people who are anorexic tend to concentrate on eating vegetables rather than other foods because they are lower in calories than meat. But perhaps you should ask why your friends are worried? If you are really sure that you are eating loads and are fine about food and that your diet is a good balance of food like vegetables, cheese, eggs, fruit and nuts, then ignore what your friends are saying or thinking. Why not check your weight on the table on* **page 35** *and see if it is within the normal range for your age?*

reLatioNships

All about
Relationships

Relationships with other people, whether family, friends, lovers or others, are among the most essential things in our lives, and time spent in these relationships can be the happiest moments that we ever experience. But also, sadly, what we may want from relationships is not always what we get, and they can be traumatic and emotionally painful as well. It takes time and patience to learn how to be a good friend and to have good friends and how to be close to other people in your relationships. The way we get good at this is by experience.

TROUBLE MAKING FRIENDS

Dr Dr Ann *I'm really shy at school and I'm moving after summer to a secondary school and I will be splitting up from my friends. I always find it hard to answer questions in class and make new friends. Got any advice?*
14 YEAR OLD GIRL.

Dear *'Shy and moving school'* – *Losing old friends and making new friends is something that we all have to do at different times of our lives, not just when you move schools. Admittedly for some people making friends is easy and it 'just happens' because they have outgoing natures, but most of us are more like you, and it can be more difficult. We have this little shell of shyness and vulnerability that we want to retreat into. So we may have to learn some tricks to help us come out of our shells. Helpful hints include trying to start to talk to people on a subject that you know a lot about. Then try asking someone you want to be friends with about what interests them. Lastly, remember that the person you want to be friends with may be just as shy as you are.*

Dear Dr. Ann, *I am black and don't have any friends as I get picked on by people who don't want to have any thing to do with me coz I am black. They also think black people take drugs but I have never taken drugs in my life and I would never take them.* **15 YEAR OLD BOY.**

Dear *'Haven't got any friends coz I am black'* — *I think what you are finding out about is just how stupid other people can be and the sort of dumb racist assumptions some people make. Don't go along with it though. You will make friends, not least because you don't and won't take drugs, and many, many people will respect you for that. Just be yourself and you will get accepted for the person that you are as long as you stick with it and maintain faith in yourself and your beliefs.*

LIMITS ON FRIENDSHIPS

Hello Ann *– I have a problem. I have a friend who I cannot name who has been friends with me since I joined my secondary school. We get on really well. But these past few months he has changed. He is very rude*  *sometimes and offensive. But most of the time he is ok. I am worried that he is using me. Tomorrow I am going to go out and buy him a present. I fear he will just take the present and leave me. I have been the victim of bullying at my school and my friend has stuck by me. But I am scared I will lose him and I will become a victim. What do I do? My mum tells me that you cannot buy friends. Please help me and reply ASAP.* **13 YEAR OLD BOY.**

Dear *'Afraid of losing a friend'* — *Although your mother is absolutely right in saying 'You cannot buy friends', an important part of a friendship is giving each other presents. But normally this is mutual in that you give each other presents, rather than it*

being just one way. This friend of yours has, in the past, been very supportive of you during hard times, and therefore this friendship obviously means a great deal to you. That fear of losing your friend means that you are giving him signals that you 'need' him as a friend rather than just 'wanting' him as a friend. When people feel 'needed' by other people this can put a strain on any relationship. I think you should relax a bit. Enjoy his friendship when you can, but try to make and enjoy other friendships too. You don't have to put up with him being 'rude and sometimes offensive' to you — maybe finding some new friends would be much better for you!

WHEN IS A FRIENDSHIP OVER?

Dear dr. Ann, *my friend at school says that I can't go to a party at his house as I am Chinese and his dad is not allowing me to go. I think my friend should stand up to his dad if he really is my friend so I don't want to be his friend anymore.* **BOY AGED** 14.

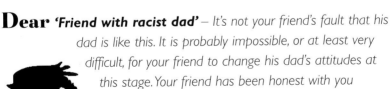

Dear **'Friend with racist dad'** *— It's not your friend's fault that his dad is like this. It is probably impossible, or at least very difficult, for your friend to change his dad's attitudes at this stage. Your friend has been honest with you about this, and I suspect he feels very badly about it all. Accept his explanation and if you like him, stay his friend.*

GETTING OVER LOST FRIENDS

Ann *– my best girlfriend just dumped me over nothing. I'm so upset. We've been friends for 9 years. What am I going to do?*
15 YEAR OLD GIRL.

Dear *'Dumped'* *– There's no way round this – being dumped by a friend is always painful, tends to make you feel less self-confident and leaves you struggling. This is especially true if the friendship was a long-term one, like yours. But life has to move on and so*

do you. Very few friendships last a lifetime, and just as you will have to get used to moving from one school to another or one place to another as you get older, you will get used to changing friendships. Changing friends doesn't always mean dumping old friends, but it does mean that we have to find ways of making new friends. You will make new best friends. Until then you have to learn to fall back on yourself and be self-confident enough to trust that better times will come again.

LACKING SELF-CONFIDENCE

Dear Doc *– I feel like a freak because I don't get the same attention as my mates and I feel as though no ladz going to like me even though my mates say they do. How can I have more confidence in my self???* **14 YEAR OLD GIRL.**

Dear *'Feel like a freak'* – *Stop comparing yourself with your mates. You are you – and the ladz are going to like you for what you are – a totally unique, one-off, special person. If you only stop worrying about it and relax a bit they will start coming to you. When they do – please be kind to them – as they may be shy and lack self-confidence themselves.*

GAY RELATIONSHIPS

Dear Dr. Ann *I quite like this boy and I'm thinking of asking him whether he fancies me but I'm quite shy and I don't know whether he's gay too. I don't think people believe me when I tell them I'm shy when asking this sort of thing. Please help me and tell me what I should do!* **16 YEAR OLD BOY.**

Dear *'Shy about being gay'* – *I can quite understand you feeling a bit shy when asking other boys whether they are gay. Even in our present world where we can talk about sex more freely, it is normal to feel quite tentative about asking other people about their personal sexual feelings. I think that you are going to have to choose the right moment when you and he are alone together. You could then start discussing the subject of people who are sexually attracted to the same sex as themselves without referring to yourself and see what his response is. If he suggests that he might feel the same way – then you can discuss what you want to do. If not, then you can back off, because you are not going to change his feelings.*

WHEN SHE IS OLDER THAN HIM

Dear Doctor Ann this may sound a bit pointless but I don't know what to do. I like this lad and he likes me. We get along really well and I think we r gonna end up goin out. The only problem is that he is a year younger than me and a bit shorter as well. I just thought it might b weird goin out wiv some one younger and shorter than me. He is 13 and I am 14. **GIRL AGED 14.**

Dear '*Liking a younger, shorter boy*' – Stop worrying over nothing – there is nothing wrong about going out with someone a year younger than you. He may be shorter than you because he hasn't had his growth spurt of puberty yet (boys tend to have their puberty a little later than girls). So watch out as you go out with him, as he may suddenly be as tall, if not taller, than you are. But who cares if he doesn't – it's what he's like as a person and how well you get on together that really counts.

IS IT LOVE?

Dear Ann – what happens when you love someone but they do not know you love them? Please answer my question it is a matter of help. **13 YEAR OLD GIRL.**

Dear '*Is it possible to love someone without them knowing?*' – Yes it's certainly possible, but how often does this word 'love' actually mean 'fancy' or *'would like to go out with' or 'want a relationship with'? Your feelings may develop into love and love is always better when it is reciprocated. People do talk about walking into a room, seeing someone and instantly falling in love with them, but I'm not sure I would call it love, rather more often it probably means that they feel a strong physical attraction to them.*

Dear Doctor Ann, *me and my boyfriend have been together for nearly a year and a half and I know it sounds silly but I think I love him too much. I'm only 16 and I don't want to be tied down but I really love him with all my heart. But I'm scared of being without him. Is it possible to be too much in love?*
GIRL AGED 16.

Dear *'Think I may love him too much'* – *Yes, it is possible to be too much in love if it stops you seeing the not-so-good, or even the bad things, about someone. The saying 'love is blind' can be true. It's great that you're happy together but you're right not to want to be tied down yet. It sounds like you are frightened of being without him and may in fact be becoming too dependent on him in this relationship. Keep your other friends. Your love for your boyfriend will be all the stronger for you being independent. Just give yourself time to see how things work out between you. People often look back to a time when they thought they were madly in love with someone and wonder what it was all about.*

WHEN IT'S YOU DOING THE DUMPING

Doc – *I've been seeing this boy for a few months now. He liked me at first & he really likes me still. He tells me all the time and says I'm perfect. But I don't feel the same! I like him a lot but I sometimes feel weird. I have my eye on someone else but I can't hurt him like that. Please help me.* **GIRL AGED 15.**

Dear *'Got your eye on someone else'* –

None of us is perfect but you will be very imperfect if you pretend that you want to be with this boy who 'really likes you'. Are you just staying with him until that someone else gets interested in you? You must tell your current boyfriend that you don't like him as much as he thinks you do. It may hurt him but it's better that he knows the truth as he'll find out sooner or later and it will hurt him even more if you let this go on. There is nothing worse than finding out that you are being taken for a ride when you imagined everything was fine.

WHAT TO DO WHEN THERE IS NO HOPE

Hi doc – *I'm feeling really depressed as 3 weeks ago my boyfriend dumped me. We got along so well and always used 2 tell each other we loved each other. Then out of the blue he finished with me. I was so upset and I still love him even though he has a new girlfriend. I cry all the time and think about him 24/7. We are still like best m8s and see each other all the time as he's in all my classes at school*

and his new girlfriend gos 2 a different school. I just really want him bk and don't know what 2 do. Do you think there is hope in the future as he does still flirt with me and says he still thinks I'm fit??? **14 YEAR OLD GIRL.**

Dear 'Dumped' – *It is always difficult to get over being dumped, especially if you see the dumper every day. He is not being a best mate to you if he is still flirting with you, even if it makes his own ego feel good. The first time you get dumped is not necessarily the worst but it is definitely nasty. Your pride gets hurt, you feel rejected and you feel that you may never have a relationship again – but you will! Ignore his flirting and go out with other friends. It may make him feel jealous – but it sounds as if it was the right time for you and he to stop being girlfriend and boyfriend. Unfortunately, it may have taken you longer to realize this than him.*

WHEN THE FEELINGS GO ON

Dear Dr Ann – *although I ended the relationship I can't stop thinking about my ex girlfriend. Please help –* **BOY AGED 15.**

Dear 'Can't stop thinking about ex-girlfriend' *– I'm not sure why your relationship broke up but there was probably a good reason for you finishing it. You may have genuine regrets and there must have been good things about this girl for you to want her to be your girlfriend in the first place. But thinking about her all the time because things haven't worked out as well as you expected since you split up, doesn't mean it would be right to have her back. It may be that you are now seeing your ex*

through rose-tinted spectacles — remembering only the good times rather than the bad. Try making a list of the good and the bad things and be realistic about why you finished it. Only allow yourself to think about your ex-girlfriend for 15 minutes a day and then gradually reduce this to 10 minutes a day and then to 1 minute until you are not thinking about her at all. Then get busy seeing other friends, making new friends and getting a new life.

NET DANGERS

Hi *– my problem is this guy. I met him on the net. I emailed him a couple of times and he's emailed me quite a few times last week. He is 14 and kept coming on and off line on the net and then he said to me that he couldn't let go. When I said why? he sed that he couldn't leave me all alone on the net. He emailed me 4 times in one day. He emails me just to say 'hi'. He once emailed me from the phone box saying hi and could we meet. I want him to be straight with me. What do you think I should do?????? Please help me. Thank you.* **13 YEAR OLD GIRL.**

Dear *'**Met on the net**' – Do not take this any further. You have no idea how old this 'guy' really is. Older men (really, really old – 30, 40, 50 years old or even more) have become experts at using the internet to persuade young girls like yourself to meet them. It is called 'grooming' and has just been made a criminal offence by the government. These men pretend to be the same sort of age as the callers they meet in chat rooms (say, 14 years old) and may even send a photo of a young boy and pretend that is a picture of themselves just to persuade you to meet them. This is very, very dangerous.*

Keep Out

You have no way of knowing the actual truth about this person, however serious and honest they appear to be. So don't be fooled or be foolish. End this 'net relationship' now and find someone your own age who you actually know from school, or from meeting through your friends or family – as long as you know them personally and NOT from the net.

TEACHERS AND FRIENDSHIP

Dear Dr Ann. *I have got a really big crush on a male teacher at our school he is about 29 and I dream about him all the time. I blush when he passes me and I really like him and want to tell him. What should I do?* **GIRL AGED 14.**

Dear *'I have a really big crush on a male teacher'*
– There is nothing wrong with you having these kinds of feelings. But you are going to have to learn to admire and like someone without actually fancying them or having a crush on them. Teachers are in a position of absolute responsibility for you and cannot and will not respond to your feelings. So my advice to you is to keep on blushing but DEFINITELY DO NOT DO ANYTHING ABOUT IT. All your teacher would do if you tell him (if he is nice about it) is explain that he is your teacher and absolutely nothing more.

QUARELLING WITH PARENTS

Dear Dr Ann *– my mum and I have been falling out with each other for a few months now and I have been getting really depressed and I have even run away once. I also feel that if I* didn't exist no one would be bothered. Please help me because we fall out over the most stupid stuff like what I want for tea. **14 YEAR OLD GIRL.**

Dear *'Falling out with your mum'* – When you are depressed it can make you feel so bad about yourself that you think no one cares. I'm sure your mum really does care, but the two of you are obviously getting cross with each other over things that shouldn't be causing trouble. Perhaps your mum is worried about other things, which are making her more irritable. Running away isn't going to sort anything out, though I am sure you only did it to try and impress upon your mum you want someone to notice you. Talk to your mum about getting help for your depression.

WHEN FAMILIES SPLIT UP

Dear Ann – our mum is divorced and she goes out all the time

and we never get to see her as she never stays at home anymore. We miss her a lot and feel that now her affairs out in the open she feels that she can do what she likes and doesn't seem to care about us anymore. On top of all that because our mum is not here our dad makes most of the rules and hardly lets us go out.

He only lets us out at the weekend (not including Fridays) and not many of our friends go out on Sundays so the only day we do actually go out is Saturday. Please can you give me some advice. From a frustrated **15 YEAR BOY.**

Dear *'Mum is divorced'* –

This must be very difficult for you. My guess is that once your mum has tasted her new 'freedom' she will settle down a bit and start thinking about your needs rather than just hers, so be patient. Your dad may be behaving in a very strict way because he is very unhappy and needs your company more since your mum left. It may also be because he doesn't know or have any experience of how much most 15-year-old boys go out. You need to find a good time to talk to him and try to negotiate a better deal about what you can and cannot do. You might suggest that he talks to some of your friends' parents to get a broader picture of what is reasonable!

WHEN FAMILY MEMBERS DIE

Dear Ann – I recently lost my Gran, Grandad and my big sister in a car crash and feel I can't cope any more. I find it so hard to talk to my mum as she is hurting too but I have nobody to talk to. Some days I wish I was dead too. I do love life but it just isn't the same without them. Is there someone I can talk to or a group who will know how I am feeling. Please help me. **17 YEAR OLD GIRL.**

Dear *'Girl who lost Gran, Grandad and older sister in a car crash'* – I am so, so sorry about your loss. Do keep trying to talk to your mother and explain your feelings because that may allow her to talk to you about her own feelings as well. I would also suggest contacting your family doctor and asking whether they have a counsellor attached to their practice who you could talk to and who would listen to how you feel. You could also try writing down your feelings because that often helps to put your emotions at a slight distance 'outside yourself' and will help you to work through them.

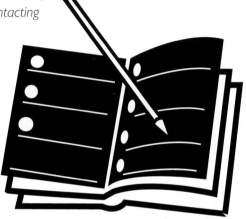

Sex

What's it all about?

Sex is much more than having orgasms and babies. OK, it is about having fun and enjoying it, but it's also about respect, trust, friendship, affection, play, love, passion, anger, making up, giggling, etc. – all the vast array of emotions you get in real everyday living.

In fact, the most important, delicious, wonderful, sexy, erogenous zone isn't between your legs – it's that hefty thing inside your head called a brain. This is because sex is always tied up with how we feel about ourselves, how we feel about other people, and how we feel about the world in general. With some people their sexual feelings are made up of pure lust, with other people sexual feelings are tied up with their religious feelings, while with other people it is linked with their feelings of confidence, but with most people it will be a combination of all these things and many others as well.

BOYS – ALL CHANGE

9–12 years (average 10ish):	*your hormones start the changes*
9–15 years (average 12–13):	*your body grows and changes shape*
11–16 years (average 13–14):	*growing fast – you grow up to a quarter of your final height during this time! Shoulders get wider, your muscles get heavier.*
11–17 years (average 14–15):	*your skin gets more oily, leading to spots.* *Your voice breaks.*
14–18 years (average 16ish):	*you are nearly adult height and build*

Dear Doc *– I am very worried about the size of my penis. I'm 15 and it is only about an inch long when not erect. i don't think this is normal for a 15 year old boy. I don't think i have started* puberty yet – my voice hasn't broken, i have no underarm hair and i have hardly any hair around my penis. I am very worried because my friend's penis is very big and he is 14. I am older and even though I haven't started puberty i think i should be bigger by now. But aren't I very late? I think every boy in my year has started to shave because they have facial hair. I have never needed to shave in my life!! Well actually if u know any way to get my penis bigger I would be very grateful. Thanks.

Dear *'15-year-old with very few pubertal changes'* – You do appear to be having your puberty at the 'late' end of normal. If you are quite far into your 16th year, then you should go and consult your doctor. Don't worry too much, because if you are slow in starting your puberty, it is unlikely that there is anything seriously wrong. If there is an actual problem, however, then you may need treatment with some special hormones that your doctor can prescribe and which will 'bring on' your puberty. Your penis will then grow bigger.

GIRLS GETTING GOING

Dear Dr Ann – I have just noticed a browny reddy colour in my knickers. I am not sure if this is my periods starting?
14 YEAR OLD GIRL.

Dear *'Coloured knickers'* – It does sound as though your hormones are gearing up and that your periods will start soon.

You may have a bit of discharge for a few months until the hormones are really working properly. When this happens, you will have a regular cycle, with your body releasing an egg from your ovaries each month. In some girls periods start to happen every month; in others they come every few months to begin with.

GIRLS – PUBIC HAIR AND PERIODS

8–11 years:	*no outside signs yet, but ovaries (the egg producers) are enlarging and hormones are at work*
8–14 (average 11–12) years:	*fine, straight pubic hairs appear*
9–15 (average 12–13) years:	*pubic hair coarsens and becomes darker, but doesn't spread. The vagina may begin to produce a clear or whitish discharge, and means a girl can expect periods within a year. Some girls get their periods – others have to wait a while.*
10–16 (average 13–14) years:	*periods start, usually irregularly at first. Pubic hair starts to grow into the triangular shape of adulthood.*
12–19 (average 15) years:	*periods happen regularly at around monthly intervals, and the ovaries start to release an egg each month*

BOYS ON THE MOVE

Dear Doctor Ann – *When I was in a P.E. lesson in Year 8, we were offered to take a shower. I did not need one because I did not do much in that lesson but most of the boys did. But they always want to look at each others dicks? Why do they do this?*

Dear *'Curious about dick viewing'* – *Boys tend to look at one another's penises, when they get the chance, in order to check out how the size and shape of other boys' equipment compares with their own – not usually because they fancy one another. It's just curiosity.*

. . . .

Dear Doctor Ann – *I have what looks like a type of a whitehead zit on my penis. What could it be?* **15 YEAR OLD BOY.**

Dear *'Person with white zits on his penis'* – *You have something in common with probably every other boy/man on the planet. Penises usually come with small round lumps, about 1 mm across, which are usually to be found around the base of your penis and the underside. These are normal 'glands', some of which will, if you squeeze them (not recommended but not particularly harmful!), produce a kind of white cheesy substance. Some, at the base of your penis, may also have hairs growing out of them.*

10-year-olds is 4–8 cm	*(1.6–3.2 inches)*
12-year-olds is 5–10 cm	*(2–4 inches)*
14-year-olds is 6–14 cm	*(2.4–5.5 inches)*
16-year-olds is 10–15 cm	*(4–5.9 inches)*
18 year-olds is 11–17 cm	*(4.3–6.7 inches)*

Dear Doctor Ann – *every time i kiss a girl i always get a stiffy and its annoying cause if we hug together when we're kissing then well you know she can feel it and i have to back off so we end up being really nervous around each other p.s. please help.* **15 YEAR OLD BOY.**

Dear *'Gets a stiffy when kissing a girl'* – *I am afraid that there is no easy way to cure this. What is happening to you and your penis is an entirely straightforward reaction when you get sexually excited. You can (a) try not to kiss your girlfriend; (b) try thinking of something like the contents of your refrigerator while your are kissing your girlfriend so as not to get too excited; (c) reassure your girlfriend that what is happening to your penis is normal, and explain that it doesn't necessarily mean that you want to go any further.*

• •

Dear Doctor Ann – *I have been circumcised and am worrying how it will affect me with girls.* **13 MALE.**

Dear *'Worried about being circumcised'* – *Don't worry about this. Most boys who are circumcised have it done as a baby for religious reasons. In fact, nearly half the men in the world have probably been circumcised and it doesn't seem to affect their sex lives with girls at all.*

• •

Dear Dr Ann – *I have an ache in my balls & i dont know what to do pppllleeeaaassseee help…? It happens when I get all sexed up.* **15 YEAR OLD BOY.**

Dear *'All sexed up person with painful balls'* – No one can explain exactly why this happens, but it is common. What seems to occur is that if a boy gets sexually excited and doesn't then have an orgasm or 'come', he may get very painful balls or a strong ache in the groin. The pain will go away within a few minutes or so (usually up to a quarter of an hour). Sometimes boys find that if they give themselves an actual orgasm by masturbating, then the pain does go. However, other boys find they actually get 'ball ache' after they have 'come'.

DOES SIZE MATTER?

Dear Ann – is there any way to make my boobs bigger? I haven't really got breasts, I've got a pair of fried eggs stuck to my lungs. **GIRL AGED 15.**

Dear *'Wanting to make your breasts bigger'* – Ask any woman about their breasts and almost all will, at one time or another, want to change them just a little bit. But if women were able to see the huge normal variation that exists in real women's breast sizes and shapes, then maybe they would change their minds and accept what they have got. Most doctors won't even consider operating on girls under the age of 18 – thank goodness – unless there are extremely good medical reasons. The breast owner's perception of 'beauty' isn't normally one of them! Before considering surgery, even if you are over 18 years old, you should look at all the other options: wearing different bras, having your bras enhanced or changed, counselling, psychological advice, etc.

VAGINA AND STUFF

Dear Doctor Ann – *I'm not sure how many holes I have and does your vaginal opening get wider when you start your period because mine seems to be very tight?! Or is this just because I'm very skinny because I do a lot of exercise??? Please help me:* **GIRL AGE 13.**

Dear *'Uncertain about number of holes'* – *All girls have three openings down below. The front one is your pee hole (urethra), the back opening is the poo hole (anus) where your body gets rid of waste faeces (turds, crap), and the middle one (a larger opening) is the vagina. The vagina is where the man's penis fits in during sexual intercourse, where the period blood comes out, and where the baby comes out when it is born. Don't worry that your vagina will be too narrow for the blood to come out when you start your periods. There will easily be enough room for this to happen. The vagina does change during puberty and it also gets wider when you are sexually stimulated and ready to have sex.*

Dear Doctor – *I am 13 and curious – what is my clitoris 4?*

Dear *'Curious about your clitoris'* – *In front of her urethra (pee tube) every girl has a clitoris. This is the female equivalent of a man's penis – the clitoris is there to give a girl pleasure, like the glans of a boy's penis! Like penises, clitorises come in different shapes and sizes, anything from a couple of millimetres to two or three centimetres. Only the front centimetre or so is* uncovered when the small hood of skin that normally covers it is pulled back. When a woman's clitoris is excited, it becomes full of blood and hardens up, rather like a man's penis, but it is still pretty small (although again, the actual size varies a lot from woman to woman). The clitoris is an incredibly sensitive organ, which is full of nerve endings. During sex, the penis pushes on the inner folds (labia) and these in turn stimulate the clitoris.

Doctor Ann – I'm just curious as to what exactly is a normal discharge? All the descriptions I've had have been pretty vague. I can get quite bad smelling discharge which sometimes looks as if it has a weird texture like jelly and it can range in colour from clear to white to a greeny-yellow colour. Is this normal and what exactly does the discharge look like when you have an infection? signed X A 15 YEAR OLD GIRL.

Dear 'Curious about vaginal discharge' – Girls start to increase the amount of discharge they produce as they go through puberty and as the hormones start to work on the cells and glands in the vagina and neck of the womb. Before puberty, most girls have very little discharge. After puberty, what is normal for one girl will not be normal for another. Some will produce a lot of discharge, whilst others produce very little. Throughout the month you will also notice it varies in colour, how sticky it is and how much of it there is. What is not normal is if the discharge becomes smelly, itchy, or greenish in colour. Any of these may mean you have an infection, especially if you have put yourself at risk by having had sex without using a condom.

GOING IT ALONE

Dear Ann – *what is masturbation and can girls and boys do it?*
GIRL AGED 15.

Dear *'Curious about masturbation'* – *Masturbation is the term normally used when either boys or girls sexually stimulate themselves. Boys usually do this by using their hand (or hands) to rub the skin of the shaft of their penis up and down. Girls normally do it by rubbing their clitoris, but may also masturbate by pushing their fingers in and out of their vaginas. So girls and boys can do it – not only to themselves, but also to each other. All this is entirely normal.*

Some boys tell me that they masturbate four, six or even more times a day. Other boys write and say that they never masturbate. The ones who do it many times a day quite often worry that they will 'run out of sperm' – and although this may occasionally happen, it is only very temporary (a few hours or so). The limit to the amount that you masturbate is really connected to the problems of making you so exhausted you can't do anything else in life, and making yourself very sore from rubbing yourself all the time.

R U READY 4 SEXUAL INTERCOURSE?

Dear Dr Ann – *I am 15 years old and all my friends have had sex. I'm the only one that has not. Should I have sex for this reason?* **15 YEAR OLD FEMALE.**

Dear *'15-year-old whose friends have all had sex'* – *This is certainly not a reason to have sex. I am sure that many of your friends have not had sexual* *intercourse yet. At 15, only one in four girls has had sex. By far the majority of girls have not had sex by the age of 16. It's you that's part of the crowd. Only have sex when you are in a loving relationship with someone you really trust and know. It is actually illegal to have sex under the age of 16, and many girls who have sex early regret it later.*

NOT GETTING PREGNANT

Dear Doctor Ann – *a boy I really trust and have liked for ages has asked me to have sex and I want to but I don't want to get pregnant but I can't talk to my mum about it because she will just tell me not to! What shall I do? I need help!*
16 YEAR OLD GIRL.

Dear *'Wanting to have sex' – You sound as if you are taking a very sensible approach and I am just sorry that you can't talk to your mum, but I do quite understand. If you are actually starting on a long-term sexual relationship with your boyfriend, you need to know what all the contraceptive options are. In order to find out what all these are, you (and your boyfriend) can either go and see your local family doctor, or go to your local Family Planning Clinic or Brook Advisory Centre, and get them to tell you about the whole range of methods available – and then you can both decide together which is the best one for you both.*

Dear Dr Ann *– can you tell me about the contraceptive pill?*
AGE: 15 SEX: FEMALE.

Dear *'15-year-old wanting to know about the contraceptive pill'* *– There are two types of contraceptive pill. The 'combined pill' is made up of two hormones – oestrogen and progesterone – and is almost 100% effective in stopping you getting pregnant if it is taken properly. It works by stopping the ovaries releasing an egg each month, so there is no egg to meet up with a sperm and develop into a baby. You need to take the pill every day for three weeks and then stop for a week, during which time you will have a bleed like a period. There is also another type of pill with only one hormone, called the 'progesterone-only pill' or 'mini pill'. This is slightly less effective, and you need to remember to take it the same time each day. Both types of pill have to be prescribed at your local GP practice or a family planning clinic. Before starting the pill, the doctor or nurse will go through all the advantages and disadvantages of the pill and make sure there is no medical reason for you not to take it. Remember, the pill does not stop sexually transmitted infections – so you do need to use condoms as well. To find out more and to obtain an excellent leaflet, contact the Family Planning Association – 0845 310 1334.*

IN AN EMERGENCY

Dear Doctor Ann *– wot is the chance of getting pregnant if u use a conny and where can u get the emergency pill from and can u take it just to be sure u r not pregnant and can some one get it 4 u – like can u take a m8s pill?* **14 YEAR OLD GIRL.**

Dear *'Conny user'* – A condom (conny) is a very good method of contraception, but it is not infallible. Sometimes it fails as a method because people take a chance and don't use one. Sometimes it breaks, sometimes it comes off, sometimes it's not put on properly, and sometimes it's not put on in time! So, lots of reasons why condoms can fail – but usually they do work very well. If any of these situations happen, you can use emergency contraception, which will work for up to 72 hours after the 'accident'. Emergency contraceptive pills are available from family planning and young person's clinics, from your family doctor or another GP – and they are free. Chemists also sell them, but usually only if you're 16 or over. Get down to one of these places as quickly as possible – ideally within 24 hours of the condom 'trouble', OK within three days, and if you wait longer there are still ways you can be helped. You should really get your own pills as it's never good to use a mate's pill.

VERY RISKY

Hi doc – can you get pregnant if you haven't had a period yet?
AGE: 13. SEX: FEMALE.

Dear *'Can you get pregnant without periods?* – Yes, you can, so never have sex without using a condom and/or other form of contraception. You ovulate (produce eggs) before your period starts and this is about 14 days before the period, and that can happen before you've ever had a period. But you absolutely should NOT be having sexual intercourse if you are **13 YEARS OLD!**

Dear Doctor Ann – *2 weeks ago I slept with my friend's boyfriend. We were drunk and didn't use protection. Because it was my friend's boyfriend I didn't tell anyone until the other day so I didn't get the morning after pill. My periods are now a week late and I'm really worried. I'm going to the Brook advisory clinic on Saturday but I wondered do I have to tell my parents if I need an abortion at 13?* **GIRL AGED 13.**

Dear *'Drunken disaster'* – *You are doing exactly the right thing by going to your local Brook Advisory Centre. Nobody, absolutely nobody likes having an abortion, and many abortions are avoidable by using the 'emergency contraceptive pill' within 72 hours of having unprotected sexual intercourse, so if it happens again, make sure you know all about taking the emergency contraceptive pill. You do not have to tell your parents about having an abortion, but although you may think they won't help you, after the initial reaction when they may be cross, they will help and support you. Talk to the people that you see at the Brook Advisory Centre about this and they will be able to advise you.*

SEXUALLY TRANSMITTED INFECTIONS

Dear Doctor Ann – *What are STDs?* **BOY AGED 15.**

Dear *'Curious about STDs'* – *These initials stand for Sexually Transmitted Diseases (sometimes also called STIs, which stands for Sexually Transmitted Infections). They are types of infections that are caught by having sexual intercourse, though some can be caught by other sexual activities. There are a whole lot of different ones, usually caused by bugs called viruses or bacteria. These include: chlamydia, trichomonas, gonorrhoea, human immunodeficiency virus (HIV), herpes, etc. If you think you might have caught one of these, please do go and get checked by a doctor. Most, but not all of them, can be easily cured and, if dealt with quickly, will not cause any damage or be passed on to other people. Some of these diseases that are caught sexually, such as thrush, can also occur without sexual contact.*

Drugs

The Low Down on
Drug highs

Taking chemical substances – whether inhaling them, drinking them, eating them or injecting them – can be almost an obsession, both for those who do drugs and for those who don't. Cries of delight on one side, and cries of horror on the other.

But it isn't all black and white. You need to look at the evidence and reach your own conclusions. Some drugs are worse than others – and it doesn't help to pretend that they are all the same. Another problem is that we still do not know what damage some drugs will do to our brains in the long term.

Dear Ann – *are all drugs bad or are some drugs good for you?*
13 YEAR OLD BOY.

Dear **'Person interested in different types of drugs'** – *The word 'drug' is used to cover different chemical substances that have different effects on our bodies and minds. At one end, there are 'drugs' like caffeine, which is found 'naturally' in tea and coffee. Then there are artificially created medicinal drugs, such as aspirin and paracetamol, which help us feel better when we have headaches or colds. You can buy these 'over the counter' at different types of shops (chemists, newsagents, supermarkets, etc), and they are safe for most people as long as they are taken in the recommended dose on the box. There are also more complicated medical drugs, like antibiotics, heart medicines, medicines to stop epileptic attacks, etc. Because these drugs tend to have more side effects, they have to be prescribed by doctors. Then there are the illegal drugs – if you use these, then you may get into trouble with the police, as well as damage your health.*

WHY THE LAW ON DRUGS?

Dear Dr Ann – *why are some drugs against the law if you take them?* **14 YEAR OLD GIRL.**

Dear **'Curious about the law'** – *Some drugs are illegal because they change the way our brain sees the outside world, and although they may make us (at least for some of the time) feel* better, happier, more relaxed, they may also make us behave in strange and unpredictable ways that can frighten ourselves and other people. Another problem is that many illegal drugs are very 'addictive', meaning that once you start taking them, you have a craving for taking more and more. Finally, most illegal drugs (as well as many legal ones!) actually have other effects which may harm both our bodies and our minds. There are some drugs that are prescribed medically – like heroin, which can be used to stop people feeling pain – but may also get used illegally without a doctor's prescription because it can also make people feel very good.

DIFFERENT TYPES OF DRUGS

Dear Dr A *– What are class A, B & C drugs?* 16-YEAR-OLD MALE.

Dear *'Drug classifier'* – In the UK, illegal drugs are classified into three main classes according to how 'bad' the illegal drug is considered to be. How likely you are to get put in jail, how long you will be put in jail, and how big a fine you pay will depend on the class of drug involved. Class A drugs are heroin, methadone, cocaine, crack, ecstasy and LSD. Class B drugs include amphetamines (speed) taken by mouth, and barbiturates. Class C drugs are the lowest class and include 'mild' amphetamines (such as slimming drugs), anabolic steroids, and valium if obtained illegally. Cannabis has now been moved from being a class B drug to being a class C drug.

WHY, OH WHY?

Doc – *why do teenagers take drugs?* **13 YEAR OLD BOY.**

Dear *'Wondering why'* – *There are a number of different reasons given by young people aged 16 when they are asked why they take drugs. There is, of course, the fact that they are easily available. Then there are the main reasons given by young people themselves: around half say they did it out of curiosity, in order to see what they are like, just for fun, etc. A third say they did it because their friends were doing drugs and they felt left out and pressurized into it. And finally, around one in five said that taking drugs was a better alternative to worrying about something else in their lives, or that it made them less anxious. Interestingly, although over three out of four young people agree 'that drugs harm your health', three out of four also agree that most young people will try out drugs at some time.*

DO YOU STAY ON DRUGS FOR EVER?

Doctor Ann – *if you take drugs once do you get hooked on them straight away?* **15 YEAR OLD MALE.**

Dear *'Worried about getting hooked straight away'* – *With some drugs like tobacco, you can be hooked after as few as four or five cigarettes, but I suspect that we are talking about the more illegal drugs here? Illegal drugs like cannabis are not thought to be addictive – but some people find that if they are taking it regularly, they become psychologically dependent on it. Another problem is that* most people smoke cannabis with tobacco and get addicted to the tobacco as a result. Other drugs, like crack, cocaine and heroin, are extremely addictive and very, very difficult to get off. So it all depends on the type of 'drug'.

DRUGS AFFECTING RELATIONSHIPS

Dr Ann – *how can you tell if someone is taking drugs? Please answer soon.* **15 YEAR OLD GIRL.**

Dear '**Wanting to know signs of drug-taking'** – People will often not be openly aware that someone else they know is taking drugs. But there will often be little changes in that person's behaviour – like them being more secretive, moody, or seeming more 'distant' – which change their relationships with those around them. Furthermore, they may smell of alcohol, cigarettes or cannabis. The most likely way to find out directly if someone is doing drugs is if they choose to talk to you about it. Another common way is finding their drugs or the 'equipment' they may use for taking certain kinds of drugs. In the case of cannabis, the drug itself may be either in the form of 'grass', which looks like dark green cut-up leaves, or 'hash', which may be green or brown hard lumps of cannabis resin. Other drugs come in different forms – ecstasy as tablets, and Lysergic acid as drops of dried liquid on small squares of blotting paper. The effects of drug-taking on people's behaviour depends on what the drug is. If someone is smoking cannabis regularly, they may appear to be rather 'vague' or 'not with it', which is why cannabis is also known as 'dope'.

SMOKING THE WHY, THE WHO, THE COST

Dear Dr Ann – *WHY do people smoke? I just think it's plain retarded.* **BOY AGED** 14.

Dear *'Puzzled non-smoker'* – *People tend to try smoking for lots of different reasons, but the main ones are:– because friends do it; because they think it makes them look 'hard'; to experiment and find out what it is like; to rebel and do something against authority; to look cool and sophisticated; to make themselves feel more self-confident; because they think it helps them concentrate; because they think that it helps keep them thin, and because cigarette companies, until the recent ban, advertised cigarettes to people in a way that was seductive and sexy. I agree that it's plain retarded to smoke, given what we know about the bad effects.*

• •

Dr ann – *People say smoking stops your penis from growing. Is this true?* **BOY AGE** 14.

Dear *'Worried about smoking and penis growth'* – *Yes, it stops you growing hard, otherwise known as impotence, though it doesn't stop your penis itself growing. It's been calculated that in the UK, there are 120,000 men under the age of 50 who are impotent (can't get their penis up whatever the size) because of smoking!*

Dear Doctor Ann – *how long does smoking take off your life?* **GIRL AGED 16.**

Dear *'Shorter life'* – *Every cigarette you smoke, on average, knocks five minutes off your life. Half of all smokers eventually get killed by the tobacco they smoke. The half who don't get killed by tobacco may still get nasty coughs and splutters, as well as polluting other people's air. The half who do get killed by tobacco lose, on average, 16 years of their life. But if you smoke and you manage to stop by the age of 20, then you don't run any increased risk of dying, and if you stop before the age of 30, you avoid over 90% of the tobacco-induced lung cancer risk. So the sooner you give up, the safer and easier it is.*

TRYING TO STOP

Dear Dr Ann – *I have tried to stop smoking but all my so called friends keep bullying me to carry on.* **GIRL AGED 16.**

Dear *'Wanting to quit smoker'* – *You're right to call them 'so-called' friends. Unfortunately, people often want support for their own bad habits by getting or keeping other people involved to make themselves feel better. The following might help you and a mate who does want to give up:*
- *Pick a day together to stop smoking.*
- *Report to each other every day about how you are doing.*
- *Work out a list of things to do instead of smoking.*
- *Consider using nicotine gum or patches.*
- *Avoid the friends who want to push you into having a fag until you feel you have really quit.*
- *Give yourselves a treat with the money you have saved.*

BOOZE NEWS

Dear Doctor Ann – *what is the limit of alcohol you should drink?* **14 YEAR OLD MALE.**

Dear *'Wanting to know how much alcohol to drink* – *There are few 'shoulds' and lots of 'should nots' about drinking alcohol. In small amounts, alcohol can be great at relaxing you and making parties go with a bang, and may even be good for your health when you are older. So, almost no one is saying don't drink at all, except for some religious groups. It is the quantity that is important – this should probably be no more than two or three units in a day, and not every day when you are 14. Remember – a unit is HALF a pint of lager, not a pint! Adult males in this sexist world can manage 21 units a week, and adult females 14 units, but if you're under 18, the weekly intake should be less than this. Any more and you're doing damage to yourself. It may sound a bit sexist, but it's just nature as boys have more water and less fat in their bodies, so they can dilute the alcohol faster. Some young people are drinking too much, and this is not only damaging their livers but also getting them involved in accidents.*

WEED – THE FACTS

Doctor Ann – *what happens when you smoke weed?*
14 YEAR OLD GIRL.

Dear *'Curious about the effects of weed'* – *Cannabis, or weed, contains more than 400 chemicals. Cannabis is normally smoked, and therefore gets into the body by being inhaled into the lungs.*

From the inside of the lungs the drugs are transferred to the bloodstream across the walls of the tiny sacs of the lungs called 'alveoli'. In the bloodstream these chemicals are then carried around your body up to the cells of your brain, where they have their effect. The inhaled chemical from cannabis that has most effect is called delta-9-tetrahydrocannobinol (THC) and different types of cannabis contain different amounts of THC. Taking cannabis also decreases your blood pressure, increases your pulse rate, can give you bloodshot eyes, tends to increase appetite, and some people get dizziness. Effects of smoking cannabis start within a few minutes and may last several hours or longer. When eaten, the effects take longer to start but may last much longer as well.

● ●

Doctor Ann – *what are the other names for weed?*
14 YEAR OLD GIRL.

Dear *'Weed word searcher'* – *There are hundreds of names for cannabis and these increase all the time. Some of these names depend on the form of the cannabis – hash, resin, grass, weed, etc. Other names depend on how it is smoked – spliff, joint, jay, reefer, etc. Some names are just names like dope, shit, draw, pot, gear, puff. Some names are from the 'East', like dagga, kabak, charas, bhang, ganga, etc. Some names are new forms of cannabis, like all the names for 'skunk', which is a hybrid form of cannabis, and include names like 'white widow', 'purple haze', 'California orange'. There are also some comic names like 'Henry VIII'.*

EFFECTS ON BODY GROWTH

Dr Ann *– does smoking weed affect your love life?*
16 YEAR OLD BOY.

Dear **'Does weed affect your love life'** *– Well, where do you want me to begin? Some male cannabis users do find that they have greater difficulties getting an erection when they are using the weed. Cannabis, whether you smoke it or take it by mouth in some form or other (like in hash brownies), can also change your behaviour so that you do things that you wouldn't normally do. An example might be getting into sexual situations you later regret, or forgetting to use condoms or other forms of contraception that you would normally use. Finally, cannabis alters the way that you sense the world – it sensitises your taste sensations and your perception of music, etc. So it may also change the way that you feel about sex – either for better or for worse!*

Dear Doc *– my Dad's a doctor and he says that I shouldn't smoke the weed because it can make me mad. Is there any truth in what he says? I daren't ask him because then he'd know that I smoked.* **15 YEAR OLD BOY.**

Dear **'Secretive cannabis smoker with doctor Dad'** *– Yes, I think your dad is right and has been reading his medical journals because there has been a whole lot about this in one of the medical journals just recently. There are basically two serious mental health problems associated with smoking cannabis. Firstly, the chances of you getting* *schizophrenia (going mad) appear to be six times higher if you smoke cannabis than if you don't. It is not yet clear whether smoking cannabis makes it more likely that someone who has a tendency to get schizophrenia actually gets it, or whether cannabis actually causes schizophrenia. But the more you smoke, the more likely you are to get schizophrenia. There does also appear to be a link between depression and smoking cannabis, but this is less obvious.*

Dear Dr ann *– my friend has quit smoking cannabis because it left her feeling down all the time. Will she eventually get back to herself. After 3–4 months it must be out of her system so if she gave it up this long could it look a lot better for her in the next few months?* **15 YEAR OLD GIRL.**

Dear **'Girl with friend who has given up cannabis'** *– Smoking cannabis has the strange effect of strengthening the mood that you were in when you started to smoke it. So, if your friend has a tendency to be depressed, then smoking cannabis will have been making it worse. It may actually cause people to get depressed. The best thing that you can do is to be there for your friend and listen to her troubles (telling someone else about what one finds depressing is a help by itself). Smoking cannabis certainly won't help her get rid of her feelings of depression but just make them worse.*

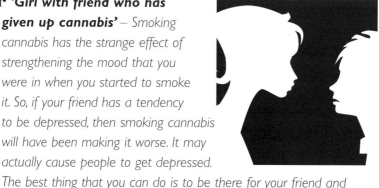

AMPHETAMINES AND SPEED

Dear Doc – *what is speed? One of my friends says I should try it but I'm a bit scared.* 14 YEAR OLD BOY.

Dear *'Scared of speed'* – *Speed is otherwise known as amphetamine and makes people feel confident, energetic and alert. It is usually bought as a white or pink powder. Speed, like other street drugs, has a large number of different names, like billy whiz, wake-ups, dexys, sulphate, uppers, ice. Technical names include Dexamphetamine, Dexedrine and Methamphetamine. You are right to be scared to try it. It is illegal, it is addictive, and it leaves you feeling depressed and exhausted.*

ECSTASY EFFECTS

Dear Dr ann – *what is ecstasy?* 14 YEAR OLD GIRL.

Dear *'Wanting to know about ecstasy'* – *It is a drug that is an entirely artificial substance. Its chemical name is 3,4 methylenedioxymethamphetamine, or MDMA for short. It comes in the form of tablets or capsules that are taken by mouth. However, what gets sold as ecstasy may be anything but ecstasy. Sometimes there is no ecstasy in it at all and sometimes there is lots – the problem is that you never know! Ecstasy itself releases chemical messengers in the brain called 5HT. This stuff normally helps control your mood – how hungry, aggressive, sexy, etc. you feel. Ecstasy made its reputation as a 'dance' drug at the huge rave parties that took place in the 1990s. Ecstasy, like most other illegal drugs, has lots of different names, like Es, Doves, essence, love doves, M and Ms, MDMA, etc.*

Need to find out more?

Teenage Health Freak
The Diary of a Teenage Health Freak
– the book that got it all going. Read
the latest version of Pete Payne's
celebrated diary in all its gory detail,
to find out pretty much all you need
to know about your health, your
body and how it works (or doesn't
– whatever).

The Diary of the Other Health Freak
– the book that kept it all going.
Pete's sister Susie sets out to
outshine her big brother with a
diary of her own, bringing the
feminine touch to a huge range of
teenage issues – sex, drugs,
relationships, the lot.

Teenage Health Freak websites
www.teenagehealthfreak.org
www.doctorann.org
Two linked websites for young
people. Catch up on the daily diary
of Pete Payne, aged 15 – still
plagued by zits, a dodgy sex life,
a pestilent sister . . . Jump to Doctor
Ann's virtual surgery for all you want
to know about fatness and farting,

sex and stress, drinking and drugs,
pimples and periods, hormones and
headaches, and a million other
things.

Other websites for teenagers
BBC kids' health
www.bbc.co.uk/health/kids

Mind Body Soul
www.mindbodysoul.gov.uk

Lifebytes
www.lifebytes.gov.uk

There4me
www.there4me.com

All your problems
Childline
Tel: 020 7239 1000
www.childline.org.uk

Alcohol
Drinkline
Helpline: 0800 917 8282
(9am – 11pm, Mon-Fri;
6pm – 11pm, Sat – Sun)
National Alcohol Helpline.

Cigarettes and smoking
QUIT
Quitline: 0800 002200
www.quit.org.uk
Want to give up smoking?
Phone this line for help.
Open 1pm – 9pm.

Drugs
National Drugs Helpline
Tel: 0800 776600
www.ndh.org.uk
A free 24-hour, 365-days-a-year
confidential service available in
English and other languages.

Bullying
Bullying Online
www.bullying.co.uk
A website that gives you lots
of tips about how to cope
with bullying.

Bereavement
RD4U
Free helpline: 0808 808 1677
(9.30am – 5.00pm, Mon – Fri)
www.RD4U.org.uk

If you are ill
NHS Direct
Tel: 0845 4647
www.nhsdirect.co.uk
Talk to a nurse on the phone
about any health problem you
are worried about.

Eating disorders
Eating Disorders Association (EDA)
First Floor, Wensume House,
103 Prince of Wales Road
Norwich NR1 1DW
Youth helpline: 01603 765050
(4 – 6pm Mon – Fri)
www.edauk.com
Youth helpline for those aged 18
and younger.

Sex and everything attached
www.RUthinking.co.uk
A great website about sex,
relationships and all that stuff.

Brook Advisory Service
Young people's helpline:
0800 0185 023
www.brook.org.uk

Index